PIANO VOCAL GUITAR

ONE DIRECTION MADE IN THE A.M.

ISBN 978-1-4950-5755-7

HAL•LEONARD®
CORPORATION
7777 W. BLUEMOUND RD. P.O. BOX 13819 MILWAUKEE, WI 53213

Visit Hal Leonard Online at
www.halleonard.com

HEY ANGEL

Words and Music by JOHN HENRY RYAN,
JULIAN BUNETTA and EDWARD DREWETT

see you at the bar at the edge of my bed, __ back seat of my car, in the back of my head. __ I

come a-live when I hear your voice. __ It's a beau-ti-ful sound, it's a beau-ti-ful noise. I

beau-ti-ful sound, it's a beau-ti-ful noise.

Hey, __

DRAG ME DOWN

Words and Music by JOHN HENRY RYAN,
JAMIE SCOTT and JULIAN BUNETTA

Moderate Pop Rock

I've got fi-re for a heart, I'm not scared of the dark. You've nev-er seen it

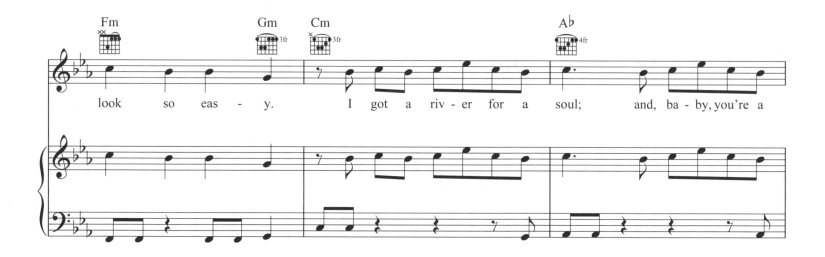

look so eas-y. I got a riv-er for a soul; and, ba-by, you're a

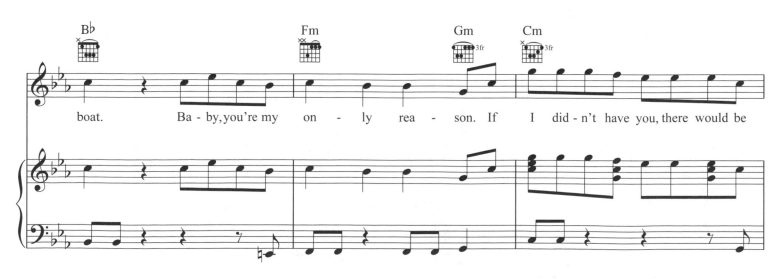

boat. Ba-by, you're my on-ly rea-son. If I did-n't have you, there would be

PERFECT

Words and Music by HARRY STYLES,
LOUIS TOMLINSON, JOHN HENRY RYAN,
JESSE SHATKIN, MAUREEN McDONALD,
JACOB HINDLIN and JULIAN BUNETTA

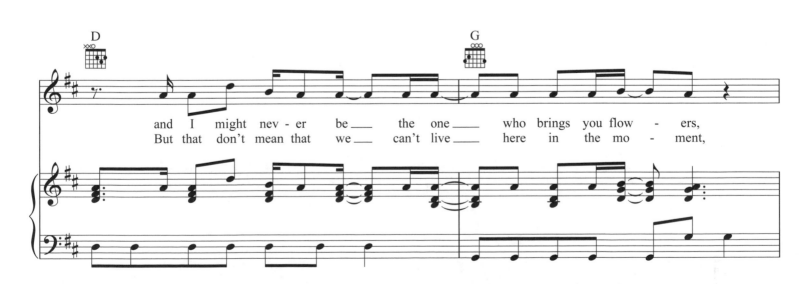

INFINITY

Words and Music by JOHN HENRY RYAN,
JULIAN BUNETTA and JAMIE SCOTT

Half-time Ballad

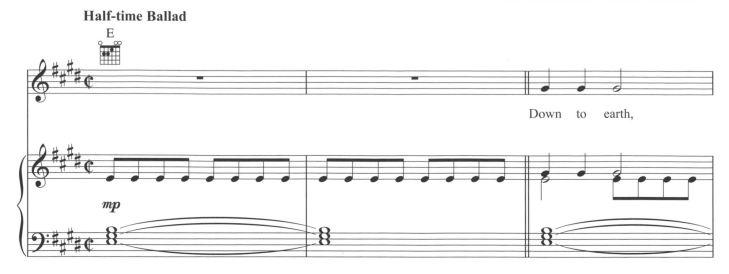

Down to earth,

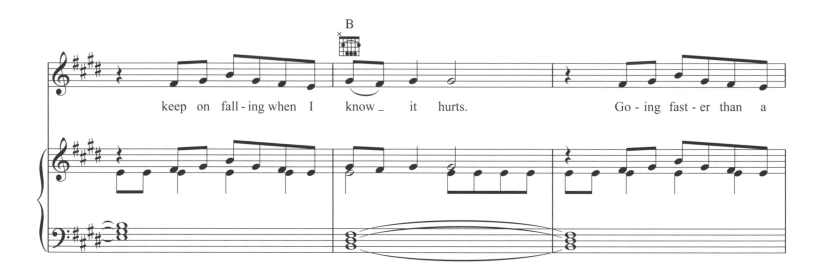

keep on fall-ing when I know _ it hurts. Go-ing fast-er than a

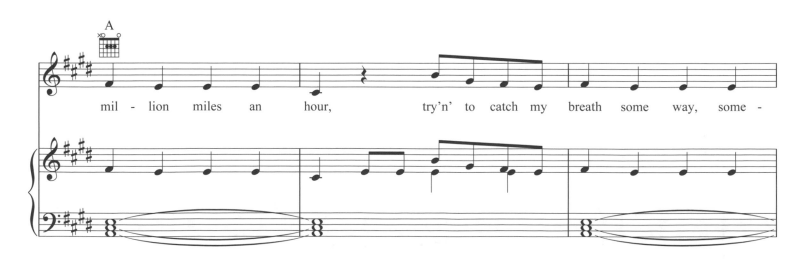

mil-lion miles an hour, try'n' to catch my breath some way, some-

END OF THE DAY

Words and Music by LIAM PAYNE,
LOUIS TOMLINSON, JOHN HENRY RYAN,
WAYNE ANTHONY HECTOR, JULIAN BUNETTA,
EDWARD DREWETT, GAMAL LEWIS
and JACOB HINDLIN

Pop Rock

I told her that I loved her, was not sure if she heard. The
said the night was o-ver, I said it's for-ev-er.

roof was pret-ty wind-y and she did-n't say a word. The
Twen-ty min-utes lat-er, wound up in the hos-pi-tal. The

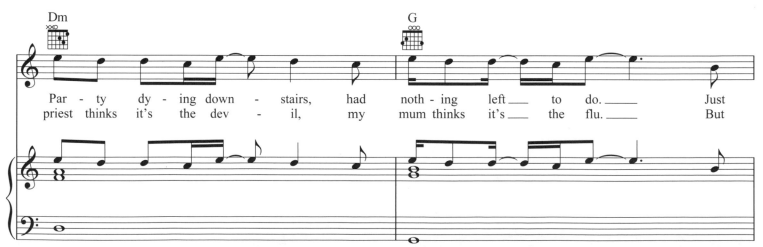

Par-ty dy-ing down-stairs, had noth-ing left to do. Just
priest thinks it's the dev-il, my mum thinks it's the flu. But

Recorded a half-step lower

D.S. al Coda

You're the one that I want __ at the end of the day. __ She
Oh.

CODA

one that I want __ at the end of the day. __ When the sun goes down I

know that you and me and ev-'ry-thing will be al-right. And when the cit-y's sleep-ing,

you and I can stay a-wake and keep on dream-ing, you and I can stay a-wake and keep on dream-ing. __

IF I COULD FLY

Words and Music by HARRY STYLES,
JOHAN CARLSSON and ROSS GOLAN

LONG WAY DOWN

Words and Music by LIAM PAYNE,
LOUIS TOMLINSON, JOHN HENRY RYAN,
JULIAN BUNETTA and JAMIE SCOTT

NEVER ENOUGH

Words and Music by NIALL HORAN,
JOHN HENRY RYAN, JULIAN BUNETTA
and JAMIE SCOTT

Moderately fast, with energy

OLIVIA

Words and Music by HARRY STYLES,
JOHN HENRY RYAN and JULIAN BUNETTA

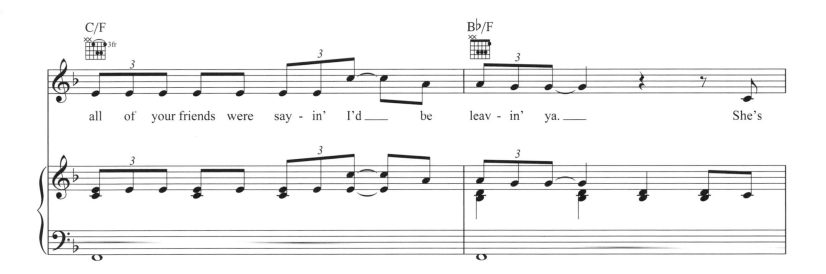

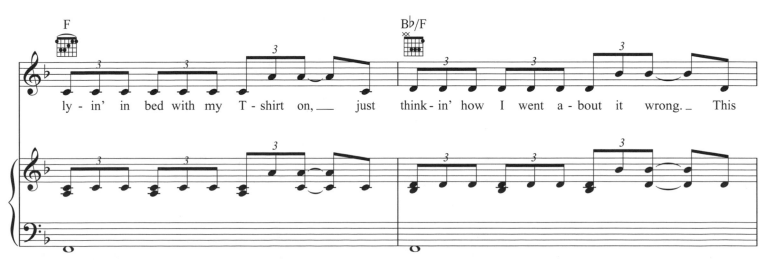

Recorded a half step higher.

D.S. al Coda

these are the rea-sons I'm cry-in' out _____ to be with ya. ___

CODA

go. _____

WHAT A FEELING

Words and Music by LIAM PAYNE,
LOUIS TOMLINSON, JAMIE SCOTT,
MIKE NEEDLE and DANIEL BRYER

LOVE YOU GOODBYE

Words and Music by LOUIS TOMLINSON,
JULIAN BUNETTA and JACOB HINDLIN

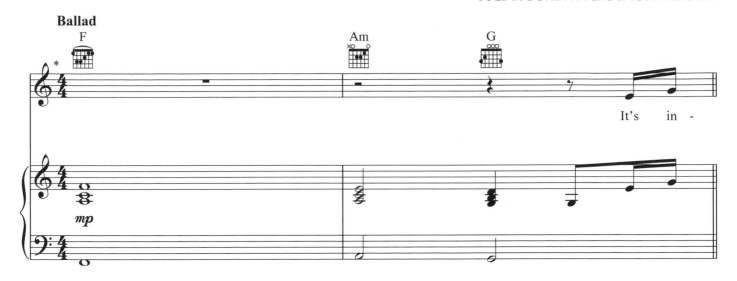

* *Recorded a half-step higher*

I WANT TO WRITE YOU A SONG

Words and Music by JOHN HENRY RYAN,
JULIAN BUNETTA and AMMAR MALIK

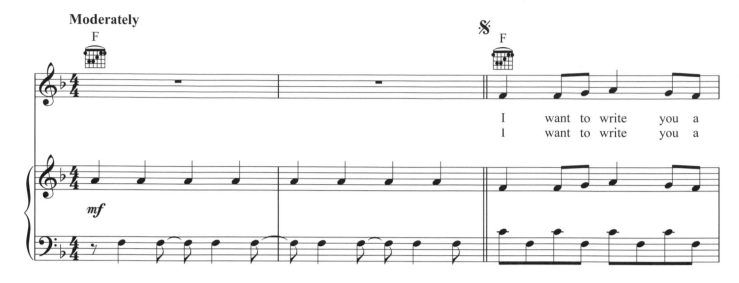

HISTORY

Words and Music by LIAM PAYNE,
LOUIS TOMLINSON, JOHN HENRY RYAN,
WAYNE ANTHONY HECTOR, JULIAN BUNETTA
and EDWARD DREWETT

Laid back Shuffle

You've got to help me, I'm los-ing my mind. _____

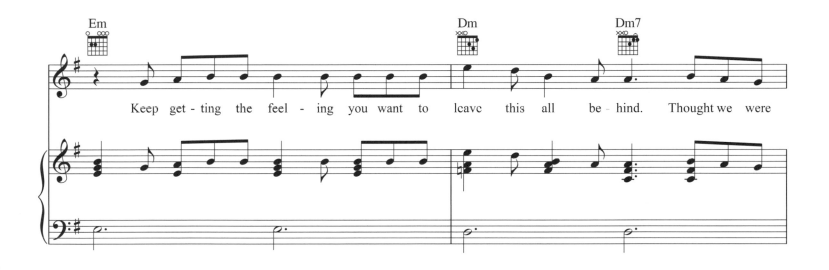

Keep get-ting the feel-ing you want to leave this all be-hind. Thought we were

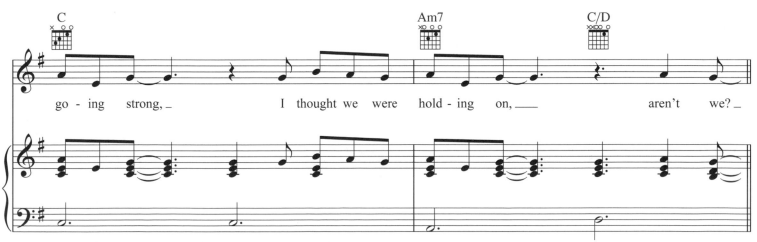

go-ing strong, ___ I thought we were hold-ing on, ___ aren't we? ___

* Recorded a half-step lower

live for - ev - er. _____ So don't let me go, ___ so don't let me go, ___ we can

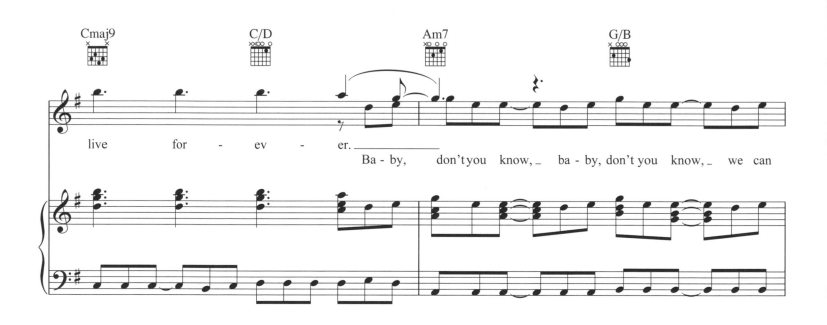

live for - ev - er. _____ Ba - by, don't you know, _ ba - by, don't you know, _ we can

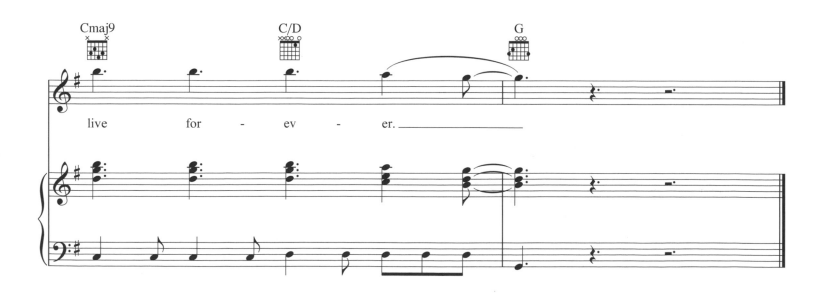

live for - ev - er. _____